What Is a Flower?

By Jenifer W. Day
Illustrated by Dorothea Barlowe

MERRIGOLD PRESS • NEW YORK

Library of Congress Catalog Card Number: 74-80883 ISBN: 0-307-03920-X   A B C D E F G H I J K L M

This is a daylily.
A daylily is a wildflower
    with large fragrant blossoms.
Its flowers form seeds
    to grow new plants.

There are many kinds
    of wildflowers.

Columbine

Dandelion

Poppy

Daisy

Violet

This is a carrot.
A carrot is a garden vegetable.
Its flowers form seeds
   to grow new plants.

There are many garden
   vegetables with flowers.

Peas

Cauliflower

Artichoke

Squash

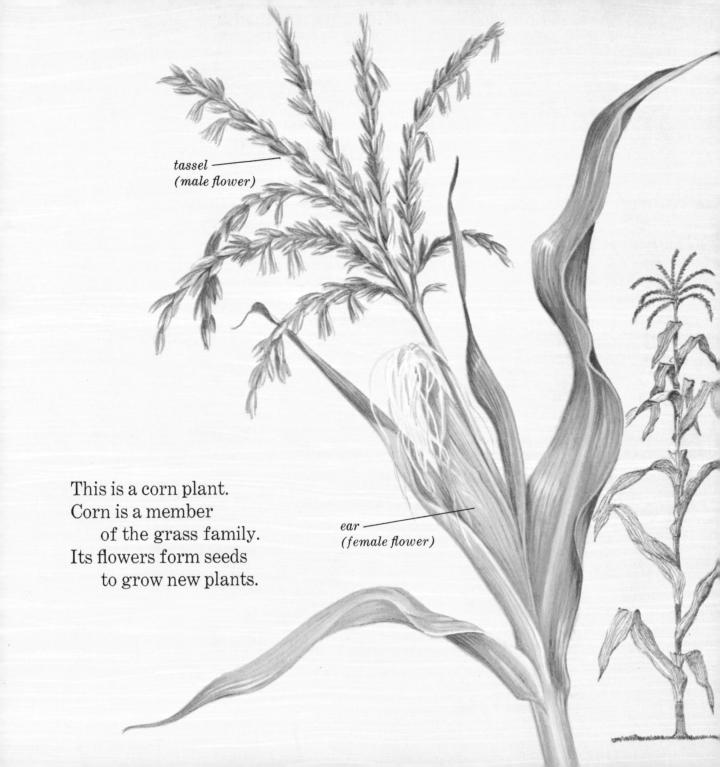

tassel
(male flower)

ear
(female flower)

This is a corn plant.
Corn is a member
    of the grass family.
Its flowers form seeds
    to grow new plants.

There are many kinds
of grasses with flowers.

Wheat

Bluegrass

Rice

Rye

This is a milkweed flower.
A milkweed is a weedy plant.
Its flowers form seeds
   to grow new plants.

There are many kinds
   of weeds with flowers.

Goldenrod

Chicory

Cudweed

Lady's Thumb

This is a flower
     from a yellow poplar.
A yellow poplar is a tree.
It is sometimes called
     a tulip tree.
Its greenish flowers are
     shaped like tulips.
Its flowers form seeds
     to grow new plants.

There are many kinds
     of trees with flowers.

Dogwood

Mimosa

Horse Chestnut

Royal
Poinciana

This is a rhododendron flower.
A rhododendron is a shrub
    that has evergreen leaves.
Some rhododendrons
    have white flowers.
The flowers form seeds
    to grow new plants.

There are many kinds
    of shrubs with flowers.

Lilac

Hibiscus

Swamp
Azalea

Forsythia

This is a rose.
A rose is a thorny plant
    that is grown mainly
    for its beautiful flowers.
Some members of the rose family
    are grown for their fruits.

The fruits come from the flowers
    and the seeds are in the fruit.

Hawthorn

Plum

Apple

Black Cherry

There are many members in the rose family.

This is a trumpet vine.
Its stems twine around fence posts,
    along fences, around other plants,
    or climb on any support that is handy.
Its flowers form seeds
    to grow new plants.

There are many kinds
    of vines with flowers.

Honeysuckle

Dutchman's
Pipe

Clematis

Morning
Glory

This is an orchid.
An orchid is an exotic plant that
    usually grows in the tropics.
The flowers form seeds
    to grow new plants.

There are many
    exotic plants with flowers.

Bird-of-Paradise

Night-blooming
Cereus

Yucca

Bromeliad

This is an iris lily.
An iris is a garden flower.
Iris flowers form seeds
    to grow new plants.
But most irises are
    grown from bulbs.

There are many kinds
    of garden flowers.

Zinnia

Hollyhock

Tulip

Pansy

This is a pitcher plant.
Pitcher plants are carnivorous.
They feed on insects.
Their flowers form seeds
    to grow new plants.

There are many carnivorous
plants with flowers.

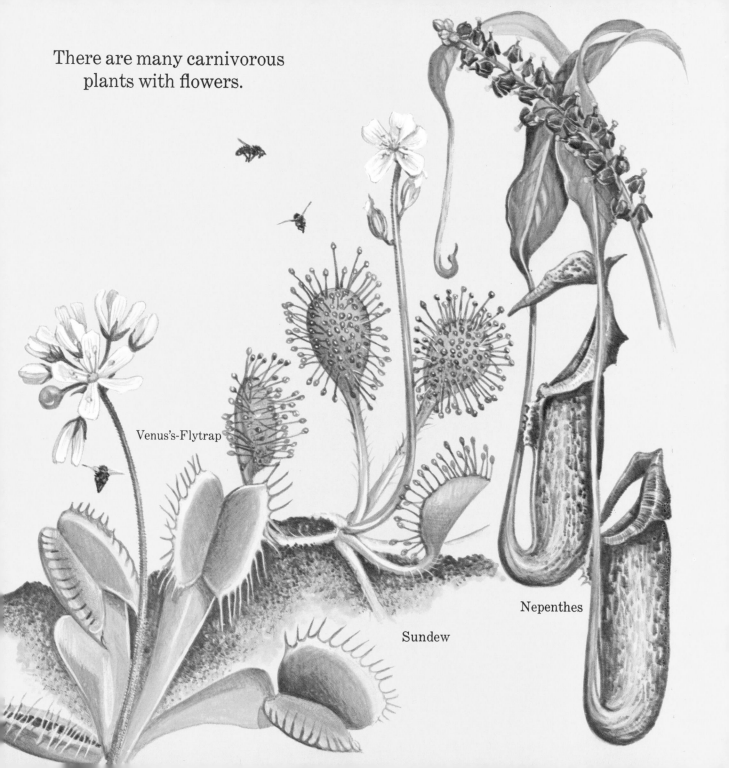

Venus's-Flytrap

Sundew

Nepenthes

But what exactly is a flower?
A flower is the reproductive part
        of any seed-bearing plant.
Weeds, vines, trees, vegetables,
        and even grasses have flowers.
There are about 250,000 different kinds
        of flowering plants. They grow almost
        everywhere, from snow-covered mountains
        to hot, dry deserts.
Flowering plants are an important and
        beautiful part of our world.